LIFE AND INSPIRATIONAL

II

JOHN CRAWFORD

Order this book online at www.trafford.com
or email orders@trafford.com

Most Trafford titles are also available at major online book retailers.

Print information available on the last page.

ISBN: 978-1-4907-6829-8 (sc)
ISBN: 978-1-4907-6831-1 (hc)
ISBN: 978-1-4907-6830-4 (e)

Library of Congress Control Number: 2015920959

Trafford rev. 12/29/2015

 www.trafford.com

North America & international
toll-free: 1 888 232 4444 (USA & Canada)
fax: 812 355 4082

Prices; there are many

One of my largest and most hurtful failures for me is not being there as a father to my son, that i have never seen face to face. You see it was a blessing when my wife became pregnant with him. As far as i knew i could never have kids due to a childhood injury. But because of my addiction and selfishness steming from not dealing with my past sooner that i did, i never got to see him being born. I never seen him crawl for the first time nor did i get to hear his first words, hell i don't even know what they were. And now because i never spoke to a lawyer to find out my options or rights, the courts took my parental rights away from me. I admit that at the time Cody was born and most of his childhood i was high in some form or other and i didn't know what i could do to get custody, so i let my son go to the state of Virginia C.P.S. I have been told that my son was adopted out to a caring family, which is good. But at the same time it also means that i have to wait until he is old enough and if he wants to, then i can finally see my son for the first time ever. But there again that is all depending on whether or not i live that long. Inside i am being ripped apart because this is what i have to deal with for the first time while i am clean and sober. While i was high i didn't have to think about the price of my addiction, now i do. And i can say this' it hurts like a m_____f___er. So much so that i want to go back to using. Knowing that MY son is out there and that i can't be there as he grows up. I've already missed too much of his life, now i find out that i won't be there when he gets his first girlfriend, his first car, his prom, and everything else in between. Doing drugs and alcohol were definately not worth the price of getting the chance to be a father to my son. I wish that i could re-do it all but i can't. I am not looking for pity, I just want you to know one of the possible prices that you could pay if you follow the path that i did. Getting high isn't worth the cost in no way.

John R. Crawford Jr.

My Being

I continually try to understand, where i am and what is to be the plan.

I try to move forward and do the right thing, but i still don't know the reason for my being.

I am always in pain in some form, and it makes me feel scorn.

I try to open doors to improve myself, but then there are attacks on my mental health.

Because of what is going on in my mind, from my true path i am blind.

I don't know if i will ever see, the path that is meant for me.

I always question why am i here, when my mind is never clear.

I try to fight my thoughts of death, but it's as though this is my quest.

Several times i have tried to die, but i'm still here and i don't know why.

Even now when i try, i ask people not to cry because one day i will be successful at suicide.

Mother Nature

As a storm draws near, most people cower in fear.

Mother nature puts on a show, every time that the winds start to blow.

In the blink of an eye, lightning brightens up the sky.

Thunder clashes as she bats her lashes.

She looks at the earth, she sees what we have done and feels the hurt.

As she starts to cry, no where is the world dry.

She sees all the damage that has been done, all by our forefathers and their sons.

With all that she does, she wonders how to make it as it once was.

With the scorched earth and the hole in the ozone, she feels completely alone.

I just can't believe, that mankind turns a blind eye, and can not see.

Love Lost

Ever since we part, there has been a darkness in my heart.

And when i think of what i have lost, i realize that it was too high a cost.

Because i have lost my heartbeat, i now only follow my feet.

Now that you are no longer mine, i have lost all track of time.

I know what i had was true, because now i can only think of you.

You sparked something inside, this to you i confide.

Even with problems unfolding, onto me you were holding.

I really couldn't see what it was that you saw in me, but it was you that set me free.

Because of you, i could do anything that i wanted to.

Now that you are gone, everything in my life has gone wrong.

I have so much pain in my life that i want to give up the fight.

When i think of how it used to be, i realize that was a blessing for me, one that i could not see.

The way i now feel inside, makes me want to die.

There is so much emptiness that for life i could care less.

I would go to any end, just to have you back again.

They say to love someone else, you must first love yourself.

But that love has left me, and i can no longer be free.

And just like the dead sea, my life is empty.

I know nothing else will ever do as long as i don't have you.

Bliss or Ripped Apart

With each word that you say, it takes a little bit of the pain away.

I get filled with passion, when ever i look at you in my fashion.

I look at you with my heart and mind, wishing that you were mine.

When i think of you, in my heart i know it to be true.

I want to tell the whole world, that you are my girl.

But when ever you are near, i start to tremble in fear.

I look at your lips and i know that it would be bliss with just a single kiss.

Behind your eyes i can see the fires, and when i look into your heart it's with you that i want to be a part.

I wonder if you feel what i feel in my heart or will it be ripped apart.

I dont know if i could ever convey what i truly want to say.

Let our hearts never grow cold, but with each other continue to grow old.

His Grace

Physically you may be in a tower, just to try and get closer to your higher power.

But in reality, to get closer it must be spiritually.

You can say that you believe, but its your heart he has to receive.

The pain that you hold on to, releasing it is what you must do.

When you flow through life, it's for him that we do what is right.

We all sin and give in, but as long as we forgive we will be forgiven.

No matter what road you travel down, as long as you believe his love you will receive.

So always pray, and in his grace you will stay.

Fires in the Sky

I look up at the fires in the sky and as i do i wonder why.

There has been so many good ones go before me, and i still can't see.

Why am i here, not knowing brings me fear.

What i am supposed to do, i haven't got a clue.

As i try to find the answers inward i search, then i begin to curse.

All i see is degredation and pain, so i know i'll never be the same.

I have found something new, but is this what i am supposed to do.

The more i open my heart, from inside the more it get's ripped apart.

I want to know the peace within and how to live without sin.

Must i go blind to see that which is meant for me.

Must i lose my hands to touch what i can not feel.

Do i have to lose my heart in order to love or lose my mind to understand.

I give myself freely in hopes that it will heal me.

Must i lose my legs to stand for what is right, or will you show me the way so that i will never stray.

I want to stand by your side and i want to do it with pride.

Help me i yell so that i can tell.

I just want to spred the word, in a way that it will be heard.

Break the Chains

Please show me how to be free, so that i can see.

Through me let the heaven's ring, so that everyone will see the beauty in everything.

Let my words fly high so that all will try and no one will cry.

Let my words help everyone to love one another, for we all are sister and brother.

Show me the way to make it a better day.

You already have my heart and soul, so take total control.

I ask that you make me your vessel, not just the trestle.

I ask for you to guide me, so that the whole world can see.

Help me to break the binding chains, so that the people of the world will change.

And if i am to be taken away, then let it be so that the people of the world may stay.

Moving On

We know it's time to move on, when our life has become stale and sad for so long.

We no longer care what happens in our life, then we stay out of sight.

We stay away from the light and only come out at night.

We knoww that darkness has moved in, as change starts to begin.

There are shades of gray, and yet here is where we stay.

Our food has gotten old, and the world has gotten cold.

And most would agree, this is not where we choose to be.

But to live once again, it's on ourselves we must depend.

But how can this be, if we are unable to see.

Never Ending Time

As i listen to love songs on the radio, i realize this is what i want to know.

For me it's not about lust, but finding someone that i can trust.

I want to be able to look someone in the eye, and see the love they can not hide.

When you are willing to give everything, that's when you can hear heaven's bells ring.

You are lifted so high that you can tell the whole world, you will survive.

It's when the only person that you can see, is the one that can set you free.

You can do no wrong, when your with the one that makes you strong.

They lift your body and spirit, so the whole world can see it.

They make you so complete, that you float and no longer need your feet.

They make you strive to always feel alive and you never want time to end so that your life with them will never end.

Free from Sin

They say to open your heart and let the lord in and your life will be free from sin.

This is what i want to believe, but in today's world it is hard to see.

With all of the pain and misery, the only pure thing is a baby.

With each other in order to live, we must learrn to forgive.

There is no reason not to get along, all we have to do is be strong.

It is easy to hate but it takes a lot more strength to forgive and let live.

Don't let pain be the game, learn to smile even if for just a little while.

Remember that we are all children of the lord, so lay down your sword.

Confusion

For a long time, i was losing my mind.

I was consumed by the dark, even when it was day in the park.

I had no feeling for what i was seeing.

I gave way to the pain, and i didn't complain.

I had a way to transfer the pain that i felt, in such a way that with it, it could be delt.

Even with all the shame, i still felt the same.

To me there was no difference in my emotion, it was all just confusion.

They all went hand in hand, this is what i had to understand.

There was but one color, and they were all mixed together.

Love and pain were one in the same.

You can't have one without the other, so why play games then run for cover.

Judgement Day

I believe that all men and women are created as equals, we all came into this world as naked babies and without sin.

We all have the capabilities to lie, cheat, steal, love, and to submit. We all have red blood in our veins no matter your skin color.

We are all brothers and sisters of the human race, so treat others the way that you want to be treated.

God wants us all to make our own way in this world.

So when you carve your own path on this earth; remember this.

One day you will have to face your higher power and you can't hide the path that you have carved from him.

Enough is Enough

Unlike humans animals are cautious of where they step and aware of their forest surroundings.

They know what they need to survive and only take that which they need.

Mankind on the other hand is never satisfied, they take what they wish and destroy what they want to.

And for what, to what end, when is enough really enough.

Will mankind destroy that which gave him life and sustanance.

And for what, all in the name of power, they will destroy one another just to say this is mine.

My Inspiration

I used to think that i have lost in the battle of love, i thought i had let my chance slip through my fingers.

But now i realize that my past was just preparing me for now.

Whenever i see you i am blinded by your beauty, my pulse starts to race whenever i am next to you.

Whenever you speak you drown out the rest of the world.

I look into your eyes of crystal and i can see into your soul, your kindness and compassion shine through as you glow.

You give me inspiration when i think of you, to me you are everything and that is where i want to be.

Aroura

I sit here with my head in my hands, with thoughts of you in my mind.

I try to think of ways to win your heart, but i don't know if it is a waste of time.

With your beauty inside you put me in a trance, and all though i want to try i am afraid that i will be denied.

I can't help but to look at you, wishing that we were two.

And when you look at me i turn my head, afraid that you will see how i really feel.

I would hold you in my arms, giving you anything that you need.

You would never have to worry because i would always be there emotionally.

You would always know that i would never go.

I would always be yours thru and thru, all i would ask is to be faithful and true.

My Soul

As i approach the dark woods i can hear the wind howl and the crickets chirp.

As i continue on, i hear mysterious and unknown sounds.

It reminds me of all the darkness an skeletons buried deep within my soul.

But now i break the bond, that has held me down for so long.

The woods no longer seem as scary or dark, as i let more love and understanding into my heart.

My path has become brighter, and with more light my soul has become lighter.

Burdens are lifted as i begin to forgive and love once more.

My past experiences have become just a memory now that i can see.

I now have a new appreciation of life and of love.

I now understand that i must love all, all of my brothers and sisters of the earth.

I realize that i was wrong, and that my soul is who i really am.

I must release all of my pain and forgive, then i can begin to live.

For the Children

There are children all over the world, and most of them can not be heard.

They live in filth and dirt that would make most people hurl. And a lot of children die just because of a lie.

We tell ourselves that i can't help, i am but only one, all the while forgetting that they too are a daughter or a son.

Yes people die every day, but it's the young onesfor whom we should pray.

Each face that we turn our backs on, could be lawyers or even doctors that could save your son.

The children are the future that we must protect, or the demons will come to collect.

And if this continues to happen, one day we will all be gone.

Being Me

Drugs and alcohol used to b my big downfall, at least that is what i thought but then differently i was taught.

Because of what i learned about me, i turned out to be my own worst enemy.

I blamed everyone for what i had done, but i was made to see that it was me.

I came to realize that i had hatred and anger inside, so with myself i did collide.

No love was in my heart or head, all along it was loathing instead.

I had to let go of these feelings, if i was ever to do any healing.

To everyone i had to show the good that i know, and now that it's me that they see i can finally be me.

Little Things

Picking trash up off of the ground, that which you threw down.

Not getting the last piece of bread, is what messes with your head.

Not getting a sweater on sale, this makes you wail.

Your mail running late, begins to make you hate.

Looking at someone cross, over a parking space that you lost.

Getting upset, just because of something that was said.

Having road rage, like an animal let out of a cage.

Why don't you realize, that your life, these things don't jeperdize.

These are just little things, so why do they sting.

We all do stupid things in our lives, just as have realized.

Damaged Past

As each day passes, i no longer need glasses.

I can finally see that whichis right in front of me.

From my past i can see the pain and sorrow, that will not be gone tomorrow.

I have caused so much damage, that in life i wish to start a new page.

I can only hope that my past will be forgiven, now that i have give in.

Because of my wrath, i have created a devastating path.

For all that i have done, long ago i should have been put down with a gun.

But now thanks to the lord, i can finally move forward.

My life is no longer a gamble, nor is it a shamble.

Inside

Love is defined as two people giving one hundred percent of themselves to one another no matter what may come. And life is always testing that love. A lot of men forget that a woman will always be stronger than a man. They forget that a woman is the heartbeat that brings forth life into this world. Whereas men are like race horses with blinders on. They forget the happiness, joy, insight, balance, and trust that women hold inside. Most men only see the beauty on the outside and not the beauty held within.

Endurance

The human endurance is amazing. It's something that you can't smell, taste, feel, or even see, yet there it is.

I've seen people live through gunshots, fatal wrecks, even fires, and they still perservere.

They go on to continue their lives without turning to some type of stimulant.

And i sit here with my addiction thinking, how can i get through this.

But then i remember the others and say to myself, if they can perservere then i know that i can.

I will find a way.

Anger

My anger got to me again today, then i said things that i didn't mean to say.

I still haven't learned control, so that it doesn't take over my soul.

I continue to work on my issues, but i still use a lot of tissues.

I know this will take a lot of time, but it feels as though I'm losing my mind.

I feel like a titan when my anger starts to heighten, but then i start to get cruel and wind up looking like a fool.

And as my temper starts to climb, it's myself that i can't find.

To control my anger there are certain things that i must learn, so that my flair up's aren't a concern.

Letting Go

The pain that you hold on to you must let go of, then you to will begin to know love.

As you release more and more, you will find yourself no longer keeping score.

As you learn to forgive, you start to live.

You don't have to forget what you had gone through, but you can show everyone the new you.

There is much that you can gain, just by learning from the pain.

Show everyone that you are now stronger, that you now shine brighter and will live longer.

All thanks to Jesus showing you how to let go.

Faces

In the darkest of light, and the coldest of night, there is evil that comes into sight.

Monsters that show their faces in the damnedest of places.

But i've realized that the most dangerous ones of all, these are the ones that we call.

I have called them forth several times, and they always do damage right in front of my eyes.

I have dark demons that i try to hide, but they always crawl out from inside.

No matter how much i pray, i have a hard time keeping them at bay.

I have yet to learn, the control for what peaks my concern.

Others may say the devil made me do it, but i seem to just say screw it.

In the simplest of terms and the easiest of way, NO is what i must say.

Forgetting to Grow

Every day we take for granted, that which we've been handed.

We continue to get older, but we forget to grow then get colder.

Why did we forget what life is, it isn't just because.

When did we forget what flowers are for, they aren't just to say i'm sorry, they are to be admired and adorned.

We think we know what love is and how to make it grow, but until you are willing to give all that you are you don't know.

We think we have control over our lives, but these are just lies.

We forget how to truly live, so we never forgive.

We don't know what it means to give, only abuse what we have been given.

I can only hope my words reach you, so that unlike me you will never be blue.

Captured

With the hundreds of women that go by, it was you that captured my eye.

Even though there are short shorts and miniskirts, it's with you that i want to flirt.

With all of my desires, it's for your heart that i aspire.

I may not have much in this life, but for your love i would fight.

Tell me what it is that i must do, so that i can be there for you.

You have become my world and my life, being with you just feels so right.

When i think of you i get this burning desire, one made completely of fire.

I have once again found compassion as well as passion.

I ask only for your love and to know your desire, then you to will know my fire.

I will show you passion in an unimaginable fashion.

You will be able to look into my eyes, and know for whom i fly.

You will know the warmth and comfort of my heart, right from the very start.

And until the end of time, you will know that you are forever mine.

To me always be true, and i will always be there to catch you.

Dead and Gone

They say that there is but one for everyone.

You have taken my heart for a ride, one that i may not survive.

In the past my heart has been crushed and ripped apart.

But with what you have done, i can no longer see the sun.

All i know is pain and misery, and from this i can't get free.

To my heart i must be true, although there were others it was always you.

For you i want my tears to flow but these i am afraid to show.

When i picture you in my mind, to myself i can not be kind.

There is so much pain, so much so that it is hard to explain.

I get so depressed that i think of killing myself.

Why do you have such a hold on me, for there is no other that i can see.

There will never be another to love you, not in the way that i do.

The pain of you being gone continues to linger on, so i wonder will it be there until i am dead and gone.

Holes in our Souls

To the people of the street, we need to become free.

We must break our binds, the ones that keep us confined.

We need to fill the holes that lie deep in our souls.

There is a battle to be won, and it's only through God's son.

The battle is not in the forests of some far off land, or even in our own sand.

The scare is not in the air, or under the sea where we can not see.

The battle isn't even in the street, but in our own heartbeat.

The battlefield is inside, in what we hide.

That's where the truth lies, so why not give it a try.

A Life Of Bliss

Is this insanity, the world that we now see is a tradgety.

We run for cover anytime fear starts to hover

We turn over a new stone, just to find that we are all alone.

If we don't create friction then things won't seem to be fiction.

We can live a life of bliss if we just remember this.

The one that wakes us up each day, is the only way.

As long as we have faith, then there is no reason to fear the wraith.

With the lord inside, there is no reason to run and hide.

We can now hold our head up high, and through life we will fly.

Being Late

Why should we be like the evil that we see.

Wouldn't life be better, if we all banded together.

Wouldn't it be grand, if against evil we all made a stand.

Life would be so sweet, if we all could be free.

Free from that which we hide down deep inside.

We know that we are not all the same, all of which comes from our shame and pain.

But if we were to let go, inside of us, a new seed would start to grow.

It's all been said before, what are we fighting for.

Is it for the all mighty dollar, or is it for the All Mighty that we holler.

All i know is that i don't want to be late, when it's my turn to pass through heaven's gate.

Coveting the Pain

I was raised to obey and to follow, but there were a lot of things that were hard to swallow.

If i didn't do what i was told, i was beaten and didn't feel whole.

I was always in trouble and at times it was horrible.

You see at age eleven, i closed myself off and only thought of heaven.

I no longer cared about anything, so i always got a beating.

Back then i was molested by someone, so the way that i felt, i only wanted death to come.

I know the person that i have to forgive, just so that i can begin to live.

It's just hard because for so long i've held it in, for thirty years i no longer cared andheld this sin.

All of it i still remember, but he wasn't a family member.

It scarred my life because i knew that it wasn't right.

I still covet this pain, and it drives me insane.

I don't want to hurt anymore, nor do i want to keep score.

I always wanted to be released from this earth, but now i believe i have found the reason for my birth.

Love from Afar

You take my breath away, every time you look my way.

I begin to shutter, when i think of you as my lover.

I know i can make you happy, but without you my life is crappy.

Having to love you from afar, is just like trying to catch a star.

When i see you with another, i ask myself why do i bother.

Then i am reminded of the sparkle in your eyes, and the dimples from your smiles.

It warms me tomy soul, then i lose all control.

Never before have i felt this way, and i can tell you, i'm here to stay.

If you knew how i feel, you would know that i'm for real.

No matter what others may say, it's for you that i pray.

I want you to know who i am, then together our lives we can plan.

Enemies

If not for my troubles i would not be who i am, i would not be humble and appreciate life in any way that i can.

I have learned through my travel that everyone has value.

I never knew or understood the meaning for my life, but thanks to my addiction and difficulties, i have gained better insight.

I have become stronger and more understanding for my fellow man.

And contrary to belief, life is not fleeting but can go by quick, so respect every man, woman and child, that is the trick.

No matter their background or their fate, just because they are different, try not to hate.

We all have the capacity to be friendly, so why make an enemy.

Blue Over You

As i watch you do your job, you smile at people as they walk by.

For me when you say hi it lifts me up to cloud nine, but when i look at you i can only get blue.

I know that given the chance i could always make you dance.

I would make you feel so high, you would never come down from the sky.

I want to grab and run with you, to where the oceans are blue.

But i know that i will never see you dance, only because you wont give me that chance.

So for now i will watch you from afar, just like i am watching a shooting star.

Creations

Why is it that all of God's creations, even the simplest of creatures such as a bird or an ant can be thousands of miles away and still find their way home.

But man, smartest of them all can not. Man was given a spirit, a brain, even a heart but still has no direction.

Yeah man can build bombs, have wars, he can even find his house, but he still can't find his way home.

Home is where the heart is, it's where love resides.

But man has forgotten compassion, forgiveness, and everything that goes with it.

Man has forgotten about God and his Son.

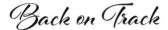

Back on Track

This morning i was thinking, i have given a big part of my life to my addiction.

As a teenager it was pot, as young man it was alcohol and pills, but my middle age was consumed by heroin and cocaine.

I realized that i have never really accomplished anything in my life, what i touched i messed up then asked why.

And when i started to dig deep down inside, what i came to realize is that i was running from myself and my feelings.

So i finally decided to stop running and to start listening to myself.

I may not like what i have to say to myself but i have to start some where if i am to ever get better.

My journey is going to be hard but living life is better than hiding from it.

Mysterious Ways

They say that God works in mysterious ways.

And i have to agree because i have closed myself off to everything around me.

I've only ever had two true friends in my life, one dead at fourteen and one still living.

I'm not saying that addiction is a good thing, but because of it, through recovery i have made some new friends and met some really good people.

So even though i was closed off, God interveened and gave me more than i have ever had.

Forgive and Forget

As i watch the dark clouds in the sky, they remind me of my life going by.

I can see my friends that are grown, they have families of their own.

I see them play with their spouse and their kids, and as i continue to watch they give them a kiss.

I watch as they buy a house and grow old with their spouse.

Their grandchildren i can see as they bounce them on their knee.

Through my addiction i sit here in place, instead of joining the human race.

I look in the mirror to see why not me, but then i realized that i don't even like me.

I still need to learn to forgive and forget, but to myself, this i can't do yet.

In The Sun

I sincerely hope that one day i will carve a path worth following.

Going from place to place i pray that others will help to pave the way.

I am but one person, but i will try to help people to listen to what i say.

I will talk to people of power to ask for help so that we can keep the children fed.

With all of the money spent on war after war think of all the good that can be done.

No child on earth would ever have to face their very last sun.

And to all of those that make millions each year, never again would a child have to cry in fear if we just listen and hear.

Think of all the victories that could be won, if you gave up just a little bit of fun, laying in the sun.

A New Friend

As i grow tired and weary my thoughts begin to get leary, but i still go on hoping that you will come back to where you belong.

As you open your heart and see what is at stake, you can see that life is too precious and short to make a mistake.

Mistakes are what most humans do and i'm sure that you will to, but as we live we learn to forgive.

When you realize that you are not alone, then you to will find your way home.

When all is said and done, in the end i hope that i have made a new friend.

A Light Rainfall

After a light rainfall, the world opens up in awwh.

When the first light begins to show, out comes a rainbow.

Birds start to sing as heaven's bells start to ring.

Angels rejoice, with the sound of a new voice.

Flowers start to bloom as the sun starts to loom.

The animals move about as the ground dries out.

Lovers hold hands as they walk through the sands.

The lord smiles upon the earth, with a new baby's birth.

No matter what storm comes around, it brings life to the ground.

It strengthens all that it touches, with all of it's small rushes.

Angels in the Sky

As angels begin to fly high, its for us that they die.

When ever the time comes, you can always hear the drums.

So when there is a storm, its evil that the angels warn.

Should the lightning have to strike, you will know the angels might and that they are ready to fight.

If they must unsheath thier steel, then that is what the darkness will feel.

Should evil look upon them, its the lord's message that they send.

So always do that which is right, or you too will have to fight.

First Seed

Is there something that you strive to be, or are you only what i can see.

Do you dream of something that you have seen, or are you only flowing through life just like a stream.

Our lives are a precious commodity, and without a purpose this you can not see.

There is a lot of beauty in the world, such as the sweet love of a girl.

So don't live with your eyees bound, you might be surprised at what you have found.

Life isn't about greed but instead what you need, so go ahead and plant that first good seed.

Day or Night

Whenever it's hot and whether you believe it or not, during the day evil comes out to play.

We all hide our many different faces, all of which have their own little spaces.

We all like to believe, that we have no evil inside like a deep rooted tree.

Even with our happy faces, it comes out in the most surprising of places.

But when our hearts have been torn, thats when it comes out in it's darkest of form.

Even if we are not agreed, we all harbor at least one dark seed.

It comes out as anger and hate, but by then it's already too late.

By then, it's a time that we would like to do again.

Broken

I have broken and not just by words spoken, but also by actions taken.

As i try working on my problems, i am told that they aren't worth solving.

It's as if i was told that i am trivial and invisible, but as long as i can breathe my life i will retrieve.

I will take back that which is mine, such as my pride and peace of mind.

I will make my dreams and aspirations come true, i won't allow myself to sit and stew.

I may have to make a huge change, but i refuse to stay the same, thats insane.

I know that my life can be better, so i want to change forever.

I will do that which is right so i will continue to fight, and i will better myself with the right help.

Flood Waters

As i watch the rain fall and the flood waters spred out, it destroys anything and everything in it's path.

That's when i realize that these flood waters and my addiction are very similar.

You see my addiction is like the rain falling down, and much like the flood waters as my addiction grows so does the damage.

It destroys family, friends, and relations; not just your mental and physical being.

Its what you do and the decisions that you make that causes the dam to break.

So remember this, when you use, there is a flood coming.

Making It

As i watch the squirrels with their families, they run, play, and teach their little ones about life.

As they scurry about for food their parents teach them what to do and what to watch out for.

And as i am feeling sorry for myself, i ask why not me, where is my family.

Then it dawns on me, i did this to myself, i chose this path of loneliness, it wasn't chosen for me.

So i have since then decided to get up off of my sorrowful butt, fix my mistakes, and make it happen for myself.

I will no longer wallow in self pitty and make a life worth while for myself, one that i can be proud of.

Change

I am told that i'm strange, only because i want to see the world change.

To see everyone treat one another with dignity and respect, this is what i expect.

To see people smile, that would make it all worth while.

To make each and every day brighter in any way, this is what i say.

We are all here for different reasons, just like the changing of the seasons.

I believe that we are not here to create pain and sorrow, but in fact to make a better tomorrow.

So i say to everyone of the world, stop hurting one another with your word.

Get rid of your evil seed, then perhaps the beauty in one another you will see.

Father and Son

As each sun rises and sets, i walk the streets thinking of my troubles and woes.

Many people i pass and many corners i turn, never raising my head to say hello.

As i walk i try to cope, but with each coorner i turn there seems to be a new concern.

I never think of anyone else but myself, i continue to wallow in self pity.

I reach my destination and do my thing, and when i finish i continue to walk with my head hung low.

I come across a dirty, shoeless, and hungry little boy, we stare at each other without saying a word and he smiles at me.

At that moment my troubles seem to disappear and i knew what i must do.

I picked him up, gave him a hug, and said, everything will be okay my son, I'm back home.

Material Things

If you want me to keep it real, then i will tell you how i feel.

I can see you in my life, with you as my wife.

I would never stray, because in my heart is where you stay.

I could tell everyone that we have a lot of fun, to me you are the one.

To you this i would say, you are the only one who brightens my day.

Any where that we go you would be admired and seen, for you would be treated like a queen.

I would open your door and push in your chair, just to let you know that i care.

I don't need material things, i just need to know that i am your king.

There isn't anything that i wouldn't do, just to keep you from feeling blue.

It is you that i boast, every time that you hold me close.

No matter the material things, joy in your life i will always bring.

Driven Snow or White Dove

You can live your whole life not knowing what is for you, but who you are is determined by what you do.

You search and search trying to find your way, so when you are young you think you know but then you start to grow.

With all of the screwing up and messing around, you realize that you started burying yourself into the ground.

As you get older, you realize that you are all alone, and there's nothing colder.

You realize that for all that you have done so far, that is nothing as compared to who you are.

You can see now that you are older, there is nothing more precious than kids and a wife.

Someone who will love you no matter what you do, and to be given love unconditionally is bigger than the highest tree.

Having love for someone is like being so high, that you can touch the moon in the night sky.

Every time that you see them coming its like your heart is humming.

Your blood is moving so fast that your fingers and toes are going to explode.

So should you ever experience this type of love, keep it as pure as the driven snow or like the white dove.

Fires

Each man and woman that lives has a fire that burns within, and each and every fire has fuel and drive which keeps us alive.

The fires that burn are for what we yearn, and what that is we each must learn.

We all hope for happiness and a life of bliss, but some burn for family and friends so that their lives will never end.

We pray for a good life so that we don't have to struggle, and at times to keep quiet we wear a muzzle.

Some things in our head we realize that the fires do burn, things that should never be said and they will always be a concern.

We know that to reach what we desire, we must control the fire.

However if we don't control them as thus, then they will consume us.

Never Give In

I know what i have seen and where i've been, and most likely it is a sin.

I have had pain arise that i keep inside, and i regret a lot that i have done and who i have become.

I have always tried to pray that it would stay forever locked away.

For i didn't want to face the demons that lay and wait.

I don't want them to ever be seen, especially now that i am clean.

But they are coming out of their hiding places, each with their different faces.

I keep asking myself what is the reason for this demon, and as i battle each one i can say that it isn't much fun.

For each and every one that i put down, there is another one that comes around.

My demons are strong and the battles are long, but some day the war i should win just as long as i never give in.

Expressions

I see many people and their faces, most of which are from different places.

It's not the way they look that intrigues me, but their expressions as they see me.

With their expressions and the way that they carry themselves, through their eyes you can almost tell.

You can see their mood just by their attitude, when they are sad their attitude is bad.

When they are happy they put on a smile, one that can be held for quite a while.

And when they are elated, you know that their hearts can't be shaded.

With each feeling that they express, you can get a small glimpse into their head.

Even if for only a brief moment in time, you should always be kind.

So just smile and say hi, it could last a long while.

Evil Spawns

As i sit here and look at the wall, my addiction begins to call.

My face starts to turn red, because i know that it is all in my head.

I don't want to give in, but my whole life that's the way that i have been.

I scrape together a few dollars, then i head from the sticks.

As i get closer i know that it is what i want and not what i need, but i still proceed.

And in my head it doesn't matter as i increase my speed.

When i get to my spot i begin to cop, and so easily the money slips from my hand as i get what i can.

When all is said and done, i don't know why i do it, and yet here i've come.

I don't want to keep on living, knowing what i am doing.

But when each day dawns, i grow stonger to stay away from those evil spawns.

Being free

I wake up from a terrible dream, and i'm shakey and trembling.

My mind is racing with thoughts, the type of ones that i have always fought.

I am filled with anxiety, of which i never thought of highly.

I have always tried to hide, from myself and what was inside.

But now my fears are coming out, with my tears and doubt.

I can see my rage and it reminds me of a lion in a cage.

From my subconcious mind, i can no longer hide.

As i get older i notice myself getting bolder, but i am learning self control as i try to fill in the hole.

The emptiness in my heart is why i want a fresh start.

I have love and compassion that i have always held within, but now my mind can no longer hold it in.

And now that i am learning to let go, i can finally try to fly free.

Carrying On

When i looked in the mirror all that i could find was that which was in my mind.

In my addiction all that i could feel and see, was me.

The only thing that i seen was what i needed and wanted, and not once was i ever haunted.

I locked things away in the back of my mindand never thought of being kind.

I knew that to myself i must be true, but in my addiction i never grew.

And now that i am sober and clean, by others i can be seen.

I have done a one eighty so now i am more trusting of lately.

I know that my demons are not dead, because they are still in my head.

But for now my demons are gone, so that i can carry on.

Back Gliding

Once again i slid backwards as one of my demons raised his evil head.

I fought as hard as i could, looked into his eyes, and there i just stood.

As he stretched out his arm and openedhis hand, i knew then, that i understand.

I knew that i could wind up dead, as thoughts raced through my head.

Should i speak up so that i could be heard, or instead take what was offered.

With first thought wrong, i emptied his hand and sang a familiar song.

As i shoved in my mouth what i knew was wrong, i could only think of the coming calm.

When all i did was to get high, i had everything taken away without a good bye.

Suicide they say is a cardinal sin, but with my thoughts i just wanted to give in.

But being here today, i am glad that my life wasn't given away.

Greener Pastures

Life is amazing, unlike any other creature we take life for granted. You see all of the animals on this planet respect and enjoy every single moment that they have on this earth. Where as humans do not, they don't appreciate that which they were given. They cheat on their spouse and beat or abandon their children, never realizing the gifts that they were given until it's too late. People continually look for that so called greener pasture when they already have it. Life is not to be ignored, because one day comes too fast, and that greener pasture that you had will be gone. So open your eyes, see what you have, and run with it. You just might enjoy yourself.

Choices

Time does heal all wounds, even those that you ensue.

Whether it's a broken leg or a broken heart, as long as you do right you will always get a fresh start.

Don't let the bad stuff get you down, or you could wind up in the ground.

The good inside of you is easy to find, just don't cross the wrong line.

You can never go back, once you commit a bad act.

You can always question what happen, just don't take any action.

For when you do, you will wish that you didn't to.

So that when the straws are all counted, you too won't be hounded.

Discover Yourself

I was watching the town of Coatesville, P.A. today. And as i watched the cars go by, i came to realize something. The people below that are going by don't even know that i am here. They can't see me nor do they know my name. But then i thought neither do i. Sure i look in the mirror and see my reflection but that is not me. When i speak i can't hear myself, i hear the words but it's as though someone else is speaking. For a long time i thought about this. I realized that, it's not me, that there was a stranger looking back at me. At that moment in time i realized that i have lost myself and that if i didn't find the person that i used to be, it would be as though i never existed. Because the person that i once knew wanted to make a difference. That person wanted to mean something, something other than hate and rezentment. So at fourty-seven years old i have decided to start fresh, to start anew. I decided that i will be someone that matters.

Desire

To know you, to hold you, and to love you, that is all i want to do.

What i truly desire, is for you to light my fire.

To be a part of your life would make me feel so right, but if you dismiss what is in my heart, it would tear me apart.

For me to keep it completely real, your heart is what i must feel.

With a rainbow in the sky, i think of you from miles high.

I am showing you what is in my heart, hoping that with me you will begin a fresh start.

But should you leave tomorrow, in my life there would be great sorrow.

I know that i am not perfect, but then again i am not a jerk.

In my life i didn't know what to do, but then i met you.

If i were just to hold your hand, then you would understand.

Blades of Grass

As i sit here in my unfamiliar surroundings, i think a lot to myself.

This is not me, this is not who i am, this person that i have become.

I thought to myself, i am just like a blade of grass.

There are thousands of blades all around me, and they are all exactly the same.

With everyone just walking by, how will i ever survive.

So unless i change to present something different and unique.

I will always be just another blade of grass.

Beam of Light

There was a time that i was filled with confusion, i looked forward in time and saw no conclusion.

All i could see were empty roads and dirty skies, in my life i could see nothing worth while.

Suddenly a beam of light broke through and my path was brightened.

My empty heart started to fill with your love and then i knew, what i was meant to do.

I am here to help my brothers and sisters of this earth, and with each word i hope to heal the hurt.

I have taken my first step on this path, and i will never look back.

Good VS Evil

When the wind blows i see the leaves dance and as it gets stonger i watch as they fall.

The trees start to bend and branches break off, the sky begins to darken as raindrops fall.

Angels start to soar as they prepare for war, and the demons down below begin to grow.

Metal clashes and blood starts to flow, God and Satan watch as evil begins to fall.

Heaven rejoices when the demons start to run, then God smiles on the earth with the coming of the sun.

You can hear the people cheer as a new day dawns, once more the world is saved with the help of God's son.

Blessings

Through my addiction i have met a lot of people and done a lot of things.

Most of which i am not proud of, or ever wanted to be, but thanks to my addiction i am now in recovery.

A lot of people would ask me why thank your addiction, for me i see it as a blessing in disguise.

I must now go through recovery, and thanks to it i have learned things about me.

I learned that i was weak mentally and couldn't control my pain.

I learned that in order to be strong, i must trust others to help me along.

I now have hope where there was none, and i now have friends that i can count on.

I now have a future to look forward to, with the help from you.

My addiction is a blessing because i also know that God and his son are on my side.

Billie Jo

Why didn't you fight, did you not believe that what we had was right.

Had you stayed, a golden road for you i would have paved; i would have given you anything and everything.

I would have made it my goal, to keep you happy right down to your soul.

I would have given you my life and my heart, just as a start.

I would have given you a home, one that you could call your own.

I would have given you love that is pure as a dove from above.

I would have given you my life, if ti would have made you fight.

Because the one thing that is so hard for me to do, that's living without you.

Grim Reaper B

There is a man with a white face, and he walks at a fast pace.

It doesn't matter if you run because he is having fun.

He comes from underground, just to see whats going on all around.

He wears a black robe and carries a scythe, thats when i shiver in fright.

I know what he has come for, but i thought that he was just folk lore.

As he starts to tear at my skin, fear surfaces from within.

When my blood starts to flow, i remember you reap what you sow.

So if your filled with hate, you will only see him when its too late.

Cody River

This one i write for my son, so that he knows he is the only one.

I want to try and help him understand who i am, so i have fought long and hard to say what i can.

I can only ask for his forgiveness, for all that i did miss.

I never wanted it to be this way, and i hope to be a part of his life someday.

He may even hate me for all that i have done, but i want him to know that he is still my son.

In his life i have missed too many years, and this is evident with my tears.

I can only say that i am sorry and hope that one day i can be at his birthday party.

And if he can find it in his heart, i would like a fresh start.

If he will give me half a chance, for him i will do all that i can.

I know that he doesn't owe me anything, but for me, i owe him everything.

End of Time

There was a time that i had no meaning or direction in my life.

I traveled a road with many curves and turns, but i always wound up in the same place.

When i searched for answers i found none, and when i looked to the sky there was no sun.

Filled with dismay i gave up all hope, but when i opened my heart, there you were.

With your hand stretched out, you lifted me up from the darkness and helped me out.

I opened my heart and even with all of my faults you accepted me, you looked past my troubles and saw the real me.

Now that you are in me i won't ever let go, i now have meaning, a purpose, and a life long dream.

Now i know, until the end of time i will never be alone.

Printed in the United States
By Bookmasters